THE NEW
NOVELLO
ANTHEM
BOOK

Forty-one classic & modern anthems for the church year.

Supervising Editor: Philip Brunelle.

Selected & Edited by Leslie East.

T0071683

NOVELLO
London

NOV 032106

Cover: "The Madonna of Humility" (detail) by Lippo di Dalmasio (late 14th century)
Reproduced by permission of The National Gallery, London.

Cover design: Michael Bell Design

Music engraving by Stave Origination

ISBN 0-85360-705-2

Second edition, 1996 (with corrections)

COMPOSER INDEX

INTRODUCTION

When, in May 1811, Vincent Novello published a two-volume collection of sacred music, he could have had no idea where it would lead. As Michael Hurd wrote, in his fascinating history (Granada Publishing, 1981) of Vincent Novello and the company that bears his name, 'what he had to offer in 1811 was a collection of music that seemed to him to fulfil a need, and which might perhaps ensure him a place among the composers he so greatly admired. His was largely a benevolent act - a wish to share the things he believed in and which experience had taught him were good and useful.'

Compiling this new anthology of anthems may not be considered such a benevolent act - though it has been a pleasant labour of love - but the aims of the collection are certainly the same. One of Vincent's own compositions (No.20) - first published from his family home-cum-shop at 67 Frith Street, Soho, London in 1834 - here takes its place among works by composers he admired and knew personally - Thomas Attwood (No.10), Samuel Wesley (No.39), Felix Mendelssohn (No.5) - in a book published from Novello's offices at 8/9 Frith Street, Soho, London in 1996. Like Vincent, the people involved with this new anthology believe that the music it contains is 'good and useful'.

The basic premise in our selection was that of the numerous fine anthems published in the 180-year period since Vincent's first issue, many are now neglected or unknown by musicians today. Within the usual limitations of space and cost we have chosen a representative sample of anthems by many of the most famous composers associated with Novello.

The next most important criterion was to reflect the fact that Novello has always encouraged contemporary composers. Composers who have a special gift for church music are not necessarily the leading composers of their time. Our selection reflects the fact that names like Bairstow, Brewer, Bullock, Darke and Harris are held in tremendous respect by cathedral and parish church choirs and their anthems have been the cornerstone of liturgical repertoire for decades. To outstanding examples of their art and craft we have added unfamiliar or completely new pieces by their successors. Five anthems are here published for the first time. Eleven living composers are represented. More than a third of the 41 anthems were written in the second half of the twentieth century. Some are very challenging, technically or stylistically, but even the most difficult have 'ways in' for the 'ordinary' choir. See, for example, how Kenneth Leighton - one of the best instances of a composer with a special gift for church music - wrote something extraordinary for an 'ordinary' parish church choir (No.2).

Finally, the choice also had to encompass simply beautiful anthems that will continue to enrich the church repertoire as long as anthems are sung 'in Quires and Places where they sing', to quote the Book of Common Prayer. Foremost among these is the one non-Novello piece, Patrick Hadley's superb *My Beloved Spake* (No.22), which, I believe, is too good to languish in an archive and deserves its place alongside the best that Novello can offer.

A compilation of this kind inevitably must reflect the judgement of one person and responsibility for the selection and the process of editing and engraving is entirely mine. In this process, however, I have been immeasurably helped by a mighty handful. Foremost among these is Philip Brunelle whose enthusiasm, not just for this project but for British music generally, is such an inspiration. Several Novello colleagues have made helpful suggestions - Tim Rogers' knowledge of the repertoire and market was especially valuable. Our friends at the Royal School of Church Music (particularly Helen Burrows) encouraged the project from the start and made helpful observations throughout. I would also like to thank Jāna Jēruma-Grīnberga and her colleagues at Oak Hill Theological College for answering some tricky queries about texts, and my 'sub-editor', Hywel Davies for seeing the book through from manuscript to print.

Leslie East
June 1996

NOTES ON THE ANTHEMS
Philip Brunelle

A suggestion for the liturgical or occasional use of an anthem during the church year is given at the end of each note. Many are suitable for a variety of occasions, however, and the classification should not be regarded as definitive or rigid.

1. Abide With Me - Ivor Atkins (1869-1953) : Organist of Worcester Cathedral for 53 years; produced the first English-language editions of major works of Bach, Brahms and Debussy, and revived the Three Choirs Festival after World War I. Elgar dedicated his *Pomp and Circumstance March No.3* to him. Rev. Henry Lyte, author of the poem, was also the first to set it to music and many have done so since. Atkins' setting, composed in true Victorian style, is a miniature 'tone poem' of the text. Don't let it become ponderous or cloying, keep it moving, giving it the dignity that it deserves. Keep the phrases legato and work on clear pronunciation. (Evening; Funerals & Memorial Services)

2. Adventante Deo - Kenneth Leighton (1929-1988) : composer, pianist and educator; taught at Edinburgh University for three decades and composed over 100 works, including many anthems for church use. All of his anthems show an unerring sense of knowing what to do with the text - imaginative, often challenging, always effective. This anthem dating from 1970 is a strong setting of a splendid text useful either preceding Advent or on Palm Sunday. Be sure to keep the rhythm absolutely firm and note that much of the anthem is two-part writing for ST and AB. A good organist is a must! (Ascension; Passiontide)

3. All Go Into One Place - Samuel Sebastian Wesley (1810-1876) : acknowledged to be the foremost church composer and the leading organist of his day being successively Organist at Leeds Parish Church, Winchester Cathedral and College and Gloucester Cathedral. Composed in 1861 for the Prince Consort's funeral this anthem is typical of Wesley's expressive and serene style when writing anthems of a penitential nature. It is in two parts - the first with unison and octave writing reflecting the solitary nature of death, and the second (in the major) in block harmony reflecting the comfort of the New Testament text. Don't let it drag; sing it with a fulsome tone giving close attention to the words. (Funerals & Memorial Services)

4. Behold, O God Our Defender - Herbert Howells (1892-1983) : composer, teacher and writer; taught at the Royal College of Music for almost 70 years and composed a great deal of music for the church as well as organ music, chamber music and solo song. His music has a characteristic modality and chromaticism which shows off his love of choral texture in a resonant acoustic. In 1953 Howells was commissioned to write a choral work for the Coronation of Her Majesty Queen Elizabeth II. He had completed the present anthem on Christmas Day, 1952, so he orchestrated it and it served as the introit for the Coronation Service in Westminster Abbey on June 2, 1953. It is just three minutes in length but those minutes give you Howells' style with its lyrical lines, grand climaxes, and fantastically soft endings. Follow his markings and the music will 'sing' itself. (Dedication services; Thanksgiving)

5. Blessed Are The Men That Fear Him - Felix Mendelssohn (1809-1847) : German composer, pianist, conductor and painter. A boy prodigy as a pianist, he began composing at a very young age (his overture to *A Midsummer Night's Dream* was composed at age 17!) and at age 20 he conducted Bach's *St.Matthew Passion* - the first performance of the work since Bach's death almost 80 years before. It was on his eighth visit to England that he conducted the first performance of his oratorio *Elijah* at the Birmingham Festival. This chorus comes from the early part of the work and needs a legato line that supports the 'peace' spoken of in this text from Psalm 112. Later on the 'light' that arises from darkness needs to have a smooth, majestic crescendo. (Funerals & Memorial Services; Lent; Marriage; Thanksgiving)

6. Blessed Are Those Servants - E.J.Moeran (1894-1950) : composer of songs, piano miniatures, orchestral and chamber music; his two late masterpieces - the cello concerto and cello sonata - were inspired by his relationship with the cellist, Peers Coetmore. Though he did not compose a great deal of choral music, Moeran has a very 'vocal' style, in part derived from his fondness for folk songs. This motet is a lovely gem that needs to keep moving along while remaining sustained. The wonderful change of key at the moment of admonition in the text needs to be kept in mind - a poignant transformation from the reminiscent sounds at the beginning to this positive change at the coming of the Lord. (Passiontide; Saints Days)

7. By The Waters Of Babylon - Samuel Coleridge-Taylor (1875-1912) : son of an English woman and a Sierra Leone doctor; was an eminent composer at the turn of the century. Though he composed extensively in all genres, he is remembered for his three choral works based on Longfellow's *Song of Hiawatha*. This anthem was composed in 1899, the same year which saw an enormous success with his cantata, *The Death of Minnehaha*. *By The Waters...* is in a very romantic style, very much in vogue at the height of the Victorian era. The important thing with this music is not to let it become overly sentimental. Give it the dignity and musical line it deserves. (Lent)

8. Christ Is The Morning Star - Michael Ball (b. 1946) : versatile Manchester-born composer, a student of Howells at the RCM, Ball has a particular gift for choral writing. This dramatic anthem demands careful preparation, especially in the coordination of the organ with solo lines. Aim for a sense of flexibility even while observing the rhythms precisely.
Text: Christus est stella matutina qui nocte saeculi transacta lucem vitae sanctis promittet et pandit aeternam (Bede: *Apocalypsum*). And he that overcometh, and keepeth my works unto the end, to him will I give power over the nations:... And I will give him the morning star (*Revelation*). Christ is the morning star who when the night of this world is past brings to his saints the promise of the light of life and opens everlasting day (translation of Bede's Latin text by Sir Roger Mynors). (Evening; Morning)

9. Christ's Bell - Alfred Hollins (1865-1942): blind from birth, he had a remarkable career as a pianist and organist. He played for Queen Victoria at Windsor when only 16. From 1897 he was Organist of the Free St. George's Church, Edinburgh where he stayed for more than 40 years. He combined this post with organ recitals and piano concerto appearances around the world. This charming carol-anthem with its bell refrains based on the chimes of Malvern depends for its effect on the contrast of verses and refrains. Make the verses move while keeping enunciation absolutely clear; dovetail the tempi and dynamics carefully at the refrains. Try not to be raucous - the unisons should be as clear as bells! (Christmas and Epiphany)

10. Come, Holy Ghost - Thomas Attwood (1765-1838) : composer and organist, a pupil of Mozart's (1785-7), held important posts at the Chapel Royal and St Paul's Cathedral and composed anthems for two coronations. His best music has a grace and charm that makes it attractive to singers and congregations. The opening of this is as effective with a small semi-chorus of one voice type as it is with a soloist. Avoid making it too static; the music must flow without sounding forced. Thinking of it as a slow dance will help and strict observation of dynamic markings will provide just enough contrast. (Pentecost/Whitsun)

11. Come, My Way, My Truth, My Life - William Harris (1883-1973) : one of those 'special' composers for the church, Sir William Henry Harris is revered by Anglican choirs for his superb motet, *Faire Is The Heaven* (1925). His ability and experience as a choir trainer - particularly at New College and Christ Church, Oxford, and then at St George's Windsor - make his choral writing naturally 'singable'. The rich tonal palette of this anthem is particularly effective when it is sung unaccompanied but choirs must be sure that intonation is secure, especially at the key changes. (Passiontide)

12. Et Resurrexit - Martin Dalby (b. 1942) : Scottish-born but educated in London (RCM) and Italy, Dalby is strongly influenced by his Scottish roots but also by a wider European experience. The coda of *Et Resurrexit...* quotes the melody and Latin words of an old Celtic antiphon for Easter Day, and the anthem's melodic and rhythmic character is clearly imbued with elements of plainsong. It is essential therefore to capture the natural singing rhythm of the set text while maintaining the *semplice* (simplicity) of approach. The harmonic surprises will then emerge dramatically and with particular potency in the quiet final section.
Translation: ("Et Resurrexit...") And He rose again on the third day according to the scriptures, and ascended into heaven, and sitteth on the right hand of the Father, from thence He shall come again in glory to judge the living and the dead, and His kingdom shall have no end. ("Crucem sanctam...") By his submission to the Holy Cross/Hell was broken in pieces/He is girded with power/and arose on the third day,/Alleluia. (Easter)

13. For I Went With The Multitude - Peter Aston (b. 1938) : composer, scholar, teacher, Aston's church music is clearly influenced by the English Baroque as well as his own firm religious conviction. His services and anthems are staple repertoire throughout the Anglican choral world. This piece shows why - a simple melodic style; the catchy Purcellian swing of the Alleluia refrain; sweetly-dissonant block harmonies; carefully-judged choral challenges. The crux of this piece is the momentary darkness of the two central questions (mm.42-49). Apart from these there is nothing 'outspoken'; take the cue from the opening indication: 'gently moving'. (Dedication Festivals; Thanksgiving)

14. From The Rising Of The Sun - Frederick Gore Ouseley (1825-1889) : an ordained minister as well as composer and scholar, Ouseley, through his founding of St Michael's College, Tenbury and the (Royal) Musical Association, brought respectability to musical scholarship and respect for the great English Cathedral tradition. His own music is classical in style but, as in this anthem, strong and direct. The 4/2 time signature should not obscure the need for a brisk tempo that nevertheless allows the climaxes to have their effect. (Christmas & Epiphany)

15. Gracious Spirit - Sebastian Forbes (b. 1941) : after studying at the RAM and Cambridge University, became a BBC music producer then a university lecturer and eventually Professor at the University of Surrey. His background as a singer and choir conductor gives his vocal music a distinct practicality. Note in this anthem that there are a few tritone intervals for each part that create a challenging harmonic language. This is a good piece to rehearse *a cappella* to check the intonation. Use the lulling 5/8 rhythm to generate a gentle cantabile. (Marriage; Pentecost/Whitsun)

16. How Beauteous Are Their Feet - Charles Villiers Stanford (1852-1924) : another composer who made an immense contribution to British music generally and Anglican church music in particular. His influence as a teacher on a whole generation of composers is matched by his fine legacy of sacred music. This piece is typical: ranging from the serenely simple opening to the majestic conclusion, it demands sensitive interpretation. The right tempo is crucial, especially at the approach to the climax. Conduct in two throughout without rushing the opening melody. (Saints Days)

17. How Beautiful Upon The Mountains - John Stainer (1840-1901) : with Ouseley, one of the most important church musicians of the late 19th century. As Organist of St Paul's Cathedral (1872-88) he had a major influence on the Anglican repertory, making editions of early polyphony and writing dramatic cantatas of which *The Crucifixion* is the best-known. Part of a large-scale anthem, *Awake, Awake..., How Beautiful...* is a sublime evocation of 'peace, that publisheth salvation'. The 4/2 metre must not be confused for a slow tempo - adjust the metronome suggestion according to the acoustic. Take care with the relative dynamics - for example, give the tenor and bass in mm.32-35 proper prominence. (General)

18. Hymn To The Trinity No.1 - Pyotr Il'yich Tchaikovsky (1840-93) : one of Nine Sacred Pieces (1885), this English version was published by Novello in 1906, reflecting the publishers' awareness of the potential of foreign composers. Tchaikovsky had become well-known in Britain with his visit to London and Cambridge in his last year. The strophic nature of the setting places attention on the adaptation: real conviction is required! The effect lies in soft singing with a clear contrast between *p* and *pp*; then the triumphant final page will sound a true song of praise. (The Trinity)

19. Jesu, Give Thy Servants/Ave Maris Stella - Franz Liszt (1811-86) : Liszt played at the home of Novello's owner, Henry Littleton on his last visit to England in 1886, Littleton having promoted the composer's oratorio, *St.Elizabeth* in the Albert Hall in 1885. This motet dates from 1865-6. The Novello version is clearly a deliberate attempt to distance it from the Marian original, making it in its two forms a very useful repertoire piece! The characteristic Lisztian chromaticisms will need careful practice and try to avoid a plodding four-in-the-bar feel.
Translation: ("Ave maris stella...") Hail, star of the sea/Mother of God/and ever virgin/joyful gate of heaven. Receiving that 'Ave'/ spoken by Gabriel/and reversing the name 'Eva',/establish peace in our lives. Loose the bonds of sin,/bring light to the blind,/destroy our wickedness,/ pray for all that is good. Be thou a mother to us:/let him, who deigned for our sake/to be born your son,/hear our prayers through thine. Most excellent/and submissive of virgins,/free us from sin, make us meek and spotless. Grant us a sinless life/prepare a safe journey for us/so that, at the sight of Jesus,/we may rejoice eternally. Praise be to God the Father,/glory to Christ the Lord/and to the Holy Spirit, the same honour to all three. Amen. (Blessed Virgin Mary; Lent; Saints Days)

20. Like As The Hart - Vincent Novello (1781-1861) : founder of the famous publishing house; was Choirmaster and Organist at the Portuguese Chapel in London. Like many of his anthems, this is hymnlike in effect, emphasising the directness of the words. Concentrate on pronunciation and phrasing; do not make it too slow or heavy or it will become ponderous; and if you have a beautiful quartet of soloists, let them sing one or all the verses - the effect can be magical. (General)

21. Mary Laid Her Child - John McCabe (b.1939) : while composer first and foremost, McCabe is an excellent example of a contemporary all-rounder : writer, administrator, virtuoso pianist. Liverpool-born, trained in Manchester and Munich, he has written in virtually every form except grand opera. This bitter-sweet little carol is a superb example of his ability to write for 'ordinary' choirs without compromising his style. Get the singers used to the 'crunches' by rehearsing different pairs of voices together. And keep the lullaby lilt steady throughout so the syncopations are more telling. (Christmas & Epiphany)

22. My Beloved Spake - Patrick Hadley (1899-1973) : known primarily as a teacher (RCM) and lecturer (Cambridge, where he became Professor in 1946), Hadley was in fact an extremely accomplished composer whose small output has real individuality. This fine anthem shows off his lyrical gift to the full, his control of harmonic progression and choral textures creating a superb mini-tone poem. Enunciation will need close attention ; encourage singers to enjoy those long, sensuous phrases. (Advent [cf Second Sunday in Advent]; Marriage)

23. O Give Thanks Unto The Lord - Arthur Bliss (1891-1975) : Director of Music for the BBC during the critical war years and later Master of the Queen's Musick, Bliss was, with Howells, perhaps the most significant Novello composer in the generation after Elgar. He had a lasting impact on the British music scene. The dramatically-charged style of his concert, film and ballet music was encapsulated with great skill in the many ceremonial pieces his official duties demanded. The march-like nature of this anthem is a case in point. To counteract the four-squareness make the most of the lyrical phrases and cross-rhythms. (Dedication Festivals; Thanksgiving)

24. O Lord, Our God, How Great Is Your Name - Anthony Milner (b.1925) : a leading contributor to the development of Catholic church music, an influential teacher (RCM and London University) and a composer of surprising passion and intensity. This dramatic, ceremonial number demands a dynamic approach, with crisp articulation and steady intonation. (Dedication Festivals)

25. O Most Merciful - Ernest Bullock (1890-1979) : a distinguished career as an educator (including Professor at Glasgow University, Principal of the Royal Scottish Academy of Music and Director of the RCM), was complemented by his distinctive contribution to Anglican church music, principally as Organist and Master of the Choristers at Westminster Abbey (1928-41). One of his earliest anthems, written when only 25, demonstrates Bullock's gift for a telling dramatic phrase (eg. mm.28-33). This drama must be captured by slightly exaggerating articulation and a fulsome tone. (Holy Communion; Lent)

26. O Quam Gloriosum - Philip Moore (b.1943) : Organist and Master of the Choristers at York Minster, formerly Assistant Organist at Canterbury, Moore is a prime example of the practical all-rounder. His instinct for choirs' capabilities is evident in this, a challenging yet joyful interpretation of a familiar text. Rehearse the fast section (mm.67ff) slowly at first, ensuring each voice is comfortable with the rhythm before combining. Emphasise the syncopations by accenting first notes of groupings and work for a warm tone at the climax (mm.114ff) - the sound is stunning in a generous acoustic.
Translation: O, how glorious is the Kingdom wherein all the saints rejoice with Christ! Clothed in white robes they follow the lamb whithersoever he goeth, praising God and saying: Blessing, and glory, and wisdom, and thanksgiving, and honour, and power, and might, be unto our God for ever and ever. Amen. (Saints Days)

27. O Strength And Stay - Eric Thiman (1900-1975) : an obvious descendant of Stainer, Stanford and Parry in his provision of practical and effective music for the church and the community. Teaching, examining and writing complemented his lifelong contribution to the church which culminated in his appointment to the City Temple in London from 1957. His gift for a memorable melody is admirably demonstrated here, enhanced by his subtle harmonic and textual contrasts in the three verses. A smooth cantabile until the final *largamente marcatos* will help the piece flow and 'sing'. (Evening; Morning)

28. Praise Ye The Lord - Michael Hurd (b. 1928) : author of several important books on English music and a composer with a real gift for word-setting and singable music. His slightly Brittenesque diatonic style is a delight for choirs. In this, the organist must carry the momentum while the choir concentrates on words and line. Rehearse the chordal passages in pairs of voices so the dissonances are perfectly in tune. (Dedication Festivals; Thanksgiving)

29. Prevent Us, O Lord - Herbert Brewer (1865-1928) : Organist at Gloucester Cathedral from 1897, he made an enterprising contribution to the Three Choirs Festivals, introducing many new works. His output was large and his concert works are probably more individual than his church pieces. This one, for instance, is typically straightforward but liturgically useful and versatile. Remember it is a prayer, one of the most well-known in the liturgy, so make the statements as simple as possible until the moderate ecstasy of 'We may glorify...' allows it to catch fire momentarily. (Holy Communion)

30. Rejoice, The Lord Is King! - Bryan Kelly (b. 1934) : a pupil of Gordon Jacob, Herbert Howells and Nadia Boulanger, and a teacher at the Royal Scottish Academy and the Royal College of Music. His penchant for Latin-American and Caribbean rhythms make his music fun to perform. It is important to avoid making the metre changes stilted - let the musical setting do its job by observing markings precisely. As in the Hurd (above) practice the dissonances between parts by rehearsing in pairs. (Advent; Ascension)

31. Sing To The Lord Of Harvest - J.H.Maunder (1858-1920) : divided his career almost equally between the church and the lyric theatre, being organist and choirmaster of several south London churches and choir trainer at the Lyceum Theatre. He wrote operettas as well as sacred cantatas such as *From Olivet To Calvary*. His music lacks subtlety but is best taken at face value and sung without sentiment. This anthem's strength is in its jolly first tune which even today has the power to send goose-bumps down a congregation's collective spine. (Harvest)

32. Sing Ye To The Lord - Edward Bairstow (1874-1946) : Organist of York Minster (1913) and Professor at Durham University, his sacred works, influenced as much by Brahms as by plainsong and early English polyphony, are treasured by the Anglican choral community. This exultant Easter anthem is full of wonderful harmonic twists and contains a couple of gloriously radiant passages of which Brahms himself might have been proud. Momentum is important whether in the *maestoso* where the rhythm has to be crisp or in the middle part where harmonies can cloy if lingered over too long. (Easter)

33. Starlight - Giles Swayne (b. 1946) : one of the most inventive and original-thinking composers of his generation, Swayne is also someone who believes in being useful. His work in schools and his direct exposure to African music helped develop an accessible melodic and rhythmic idiom that is used consistently throughout his output from the early 1980s. This carol started out for unison voices only and one might experiment with a solo (child's?) voice in verse one. Sing as smoothly as possible letting the accompaniment provide the momentum. (Christmas & Epiphany)

34. They Are At Rest - Edward Elgar (1857-1934) : unquestionably the most important late Victorian, early-twentieth century British composer. His reputation is built upon the masterpieces written between the ages of 40 and 62; his early output is vast but uneven and much of his small-scale choral music dates from that period. This anthem is an exception. Taking an inspirational poem by Cardinal Newman - as Elgar also did, of course, in *The Dream of Gerontius* - he has fashioned a hauntingly beautiful memorial piece, full of subtle word-painting. Clear enunciation is vital. (Funerals & Memorial Services)

35. They Are Happy - John Joubert (b. 1927) : while of South African origin, his style has grown from distinctive British roots. Works in all genres have established a reputation for distinctively melodic, 'vocal' writing. The parts-in-thirds writing is utterly characteristic, producing gentle dissonances that, along with the two-against-three rhythms, motivates the music's progression. In this the organist has an important role, providing decorative counterpoint at first and then later a firm metrical foundation. (Ascension; Marriage)

36. This Is The Voice - Stephen Oliver (1950-92) : an artist of rich intelligence, renowned for a natural and innovative gift for theatrical composition. Throughout his output his choral writing is particularly striking. His setting of Walter Hilton's short text is typical: exploiting a resonant acoustic, utilising limited resources to great effect, writing a splendidly busy organ part that is not as difficult as it looks, and subtly hammering home a single heartfelt message. Experiment with voice combinations especially from m.151ff. In the slow build-up to the end, precise rhythm is important. (The Trinity [cf First Sunday after Trinity])

37. Thou Art The Way - Christopher Steel (1939-1992) : studies at the RAM and in Munich were followed by a teaching career in England that led naturally to composition for both professional and amateur resources. All his music has a lightness of touch and shows a sure melodic gift. This anthem is a good example: a seemingly-simple melody is made more memorable and distinctive by the unexpectedness of the metrical and harmonic context. Note carefully the composer's directions and try to make the tempo fluctuations feel natural. (Passiontide)

38. Thou Wilt Keep Him In Perfect Peace - Robert Walker (b. 1946) : his formative musical experiences came from his time as a chorister at St Matthew's Church, Northampton, and then as a choral scholar and later organ scholar at Jesus College, Cambridge. He has written effective service settings for Norwich and Westminster Cathedrals. A sensitivity for word-setting and flexibility of vocal rhythm mark Walker's choral music. In this anthem there is a clever balance of repose and ecstatic movement, reflecting the import of the words. The fanfare-like passages (mm.26ff.) require careful line-by-line practice before combining. (Dedication Festivals; Ordination)

39. Tu Es Sacerdos - Samuel Wesley (1766-1837) : was Vincent Novello's assistant at the Portuguese Embassy Chapel when this was written. He was a gifted and versatile musician but establishment posts eluded him. A central figure in the Bach revival in England, his choral music is strongly influenced by Bachian counterpoint. This demanding little motet combines baroque texture and figuration with distinctly 19th-century harmonic fingerprints. Notice that it does not need to go fast. Practice each part slowly in precise rhythm at first. Note the single dynamic contrast at m.25 but grade the dynamics of the contrapuntal entries so that the passage from m.28 is the first true *forte tutti*.
Translation: Thou art a Priest forever after the order of Melchizedech. (Ordination)

40. View Me, Lord - Richard H. Lloyd (b.1933): Organ Scholar of Jesus College, Cambridge; Assistant Organist of Salisbury Cathedral; Organist of Hereford from 1966 and of Durham from 1974. Responsible for strengthening the Hereford contingent in the Three Choirs Festival, Lloyd also made a mark with his commissioning of several successful new choral works from contemporary composers. His service settings and *Preces and Responses* are widely used. This is a fine example of a perennially useful, simple but effective anthem, presenting text without frills or complications, letting the message come across through the memorable melodic line and natural harmonic rhythm. Make the most of the subtle change of character in verse 3. (Holy Communion; Passiontide)

41. When Christ Was Born - Harold Darke (1888-1976) : a student of Parrott and Stanford at the RCM, Darke held the post of Organist at St Michael's, Cornhill in the City of London for 50 years from 1916. Famed for his masterly setting of *In The Bleak Midwinter*, he had an unfailing gift for singable, flowing lines. The dazzling contrapuntal explosion of the refrain gives this carol a wonderful 'lift' reinforcing the almost folksong-like character of the solo verse. Indeed, verses 2 and 3 could be sung solo - soprano in 2 and tenor in 3. (Christmas & Epiphany)

ABIDE WITH ME

(An Evening Anthem)

Text
H.F. Lyte

IVOR ATKINS
(1869 - 1953)

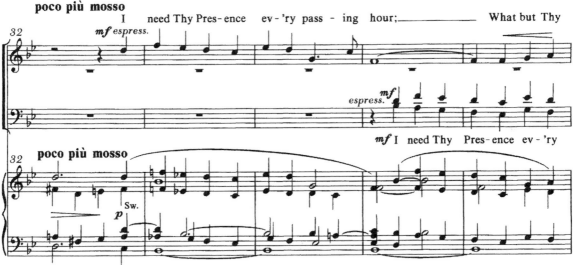

4

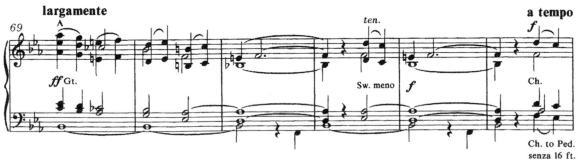

For David Patrick and the Choir of Barnet Parish Church

ADVENTANTE DEO

(Lift Up Your Heads, Gates Of My Heart)

Text
John Addington Symonds
(1840 - 93)

KENNETH LEIGHTON
(1929 - 88)

lift up your heads,

sempre marcato

lift up your heads,———————— gates— of my heart,————

to sa - lute————

un - fold Your por - tals————————

to sa - lute————

to sa - lute————

un - fold Your por - tals————————

to sa - lute————

Ped.

son eyes____ and grail____ of gold!

Be-hold him come,____

-hold Him come,____ borne____ on che-ru - bic wings____

borne__ on che - ru - bic wings

En -

En-grained with crim - son eyes____ and grail of

- grained with crim - son eyes____ and grail of gold!____

fa   thomed,   bliss_____ un

- told._____

18

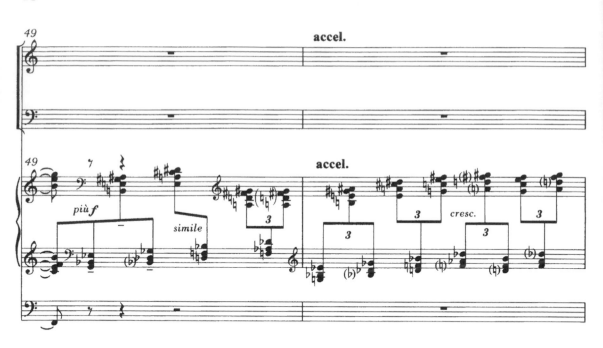

24

ALL GO UNTO ONE PLACE
(Funeral and Memorial Services)

Text
Ecclesiastes iii, 20
Psalm xxxix, 8
Ecclesiastes xii, 7
II Corinthians i, 9
II Corinthians v, 1
I Thessalonians iv, 18

SAMUEL SEBASTIAN WESLEY
(1810 -76)
Edited by W.G. Alcock

28

BEHOLD, O GOD OUR DEFENDER

Text
Psalm lxxxiv, 9-10

HERBERT HOWELLS
(1892-1983)

10
ff
- hold, O God our de-
ff
sonore
- hold, be - hold, O God our de-
f
ff
sonore
be-hold, be - hold, O God our de-
ff
- hold, O God our de-
10
ff ma dolce
f assai sonore
15
mf
p
mp
cresc. sempre
- fen - der, and look,
mf
p
mp
- fen - der, and look,
mf
p
mp
cresc. sempre mf
- fen - der, and look, and
mf
p
mp
- fen - der, and look,
15
mp
cresc. sempre

Christmas Day, 1952

BLESSED ARE THE MEN WHO FEAR HIM

(from *Elijah*)

Text
Psalm cxii, 1,4

(derived from the Lutheran Bible by
Julius Schubring,
English version by
William Bartholemew)

FELIX MENDELSSOHN
(1809-47)
(Edited by Michael Pilkington)

The accompaniment is presumed to be Mendelssohn's own as it is virtually identical to the Simrock and Ewer vocal scores.

† Choirs may prefer to sing "... are all those who ...".

© Copyright 1991, 1996 Novello & Company Limited

*Sop: ♩. ♪| (Ewer 1852) † Bass: ♩ | (Ewer 1852)
ev - er   they

*Sop: light. He is (Ewer)

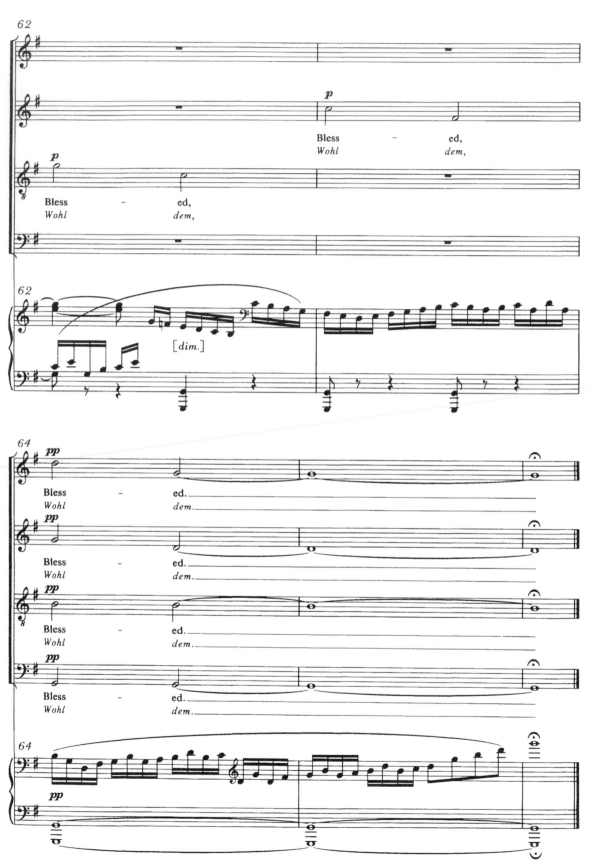

BLESSED ARE THOSE SERVANTS

Text
Luke xii, 37, 38, 40

E.J. MOERAN
(1894 - 1950)

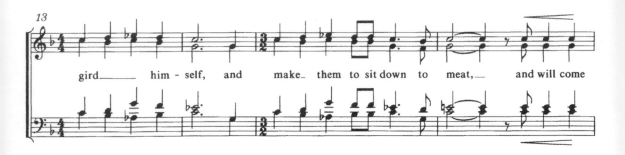

gird_____ him - self, and make_ them to sit down to meat,___ and will come

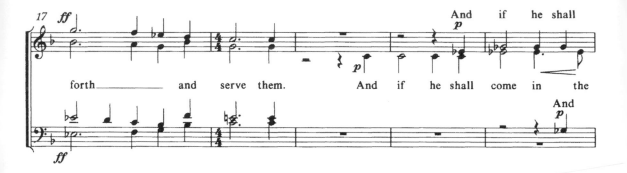

forth_____ and serve them. And if he shall come in the

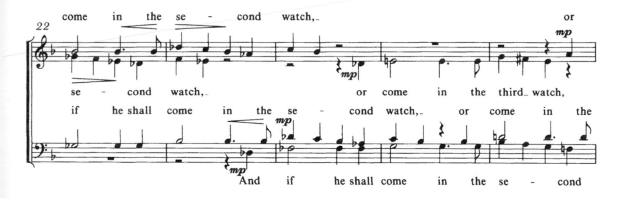

come in the se - cond watch,_ or

se - cond watch,_ or come in the third_ watch,

if he shall come in the se - cond watch,_ or come in the

And if he shall come in the se - cond

come in the third_ watch, and find_____ them so,____

and find,___ and find_____ them so,___

third_ watch, and find_____ them so,___

watch,_ or come in the third_ watch, and find them so,___

BY THE WATERS OF BABYLON

Text
Psalm cxxxvii

SAMUEL COLERIDGE-TAYLOR
(1875-1912)

Sing_ us one_ of the songs_ of_ Si - on,_ sing us one of the

songs of Si - on.__ How shall we sing_ the Lord's_ song,_ in a

strange land?___

poco rit.

poco rit.

Man.

in the day of Je-ru-sa-lem, how they said, Down with it,

down with it, e-ven to the ground.

Tempo primo

O— daugh-ter of Ba-by-lon, wast — ed with mi-se-ry, hap — py shall be

yea, hap-py shall he

Ba-by-lon, wast - ed with mi-se-ry, yea, hap-py shall he

Man.

CHRIST IS THE MORNING STAR

Text
Bede *Apocalypsum;*
Revelation ii, 26, 28;
English translation of Bede
Apocalypsum by
Roger Mynors

MICHAEL BALL
(b. 1946)

First performed on 1st July 1989 during Evensong by the choir of Manchester Cathedral with Gordon Stewart (organ), conducted by Stuart Beer, during the 1989 Festival of the Federation of Cathedral Old Choristers' Associations which commissioned the work.

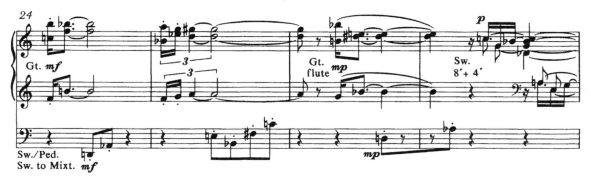

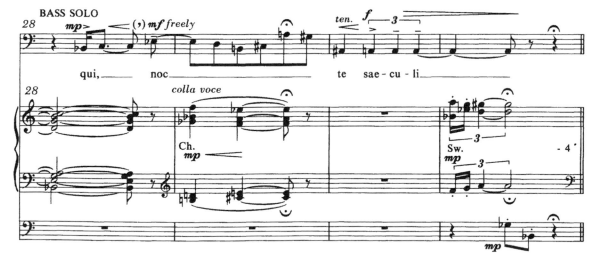

*At this point the balance of tone should allow the organ to engulf the voices.

power,_____

I will give   power,_____   I will give   power_____   o -

- ver   the   na   -   -   tions:

and   to him   that o - ver-com - eth, and   to him   that o - ver-com - eth,

64

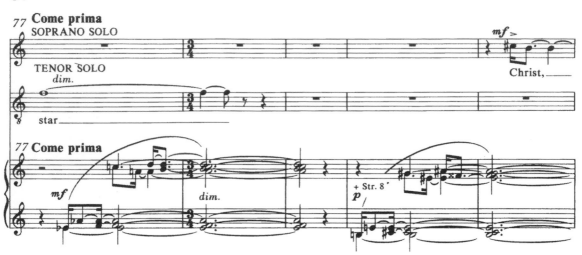

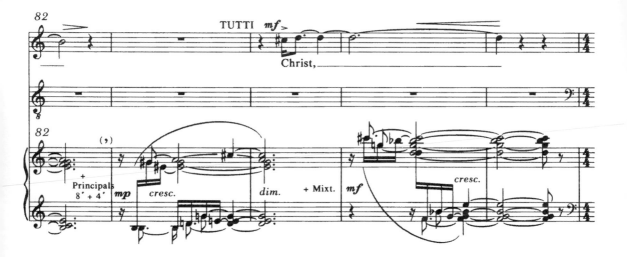

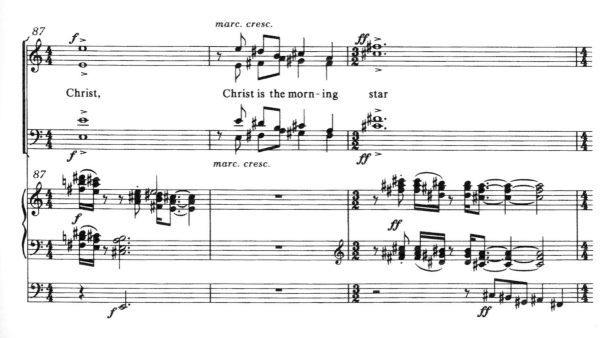

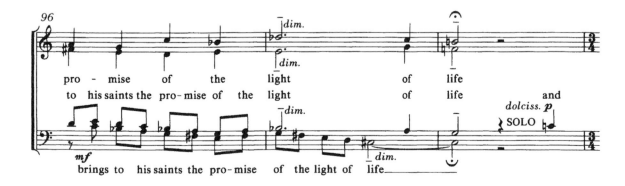

* Ideally, the soloist should leave the main choir after bar 96 and sing this final passage from a side chapel or perhaps behind the altar screen, preferably singing with his back to the congregation to distance the sound as much as possible.

Chris - tus____ est____ stel - la____

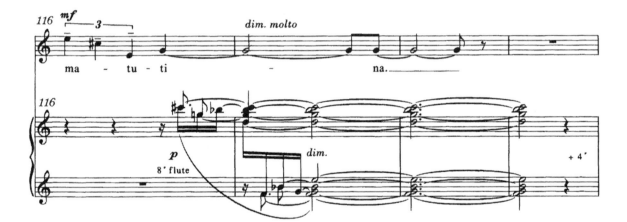

ma - tu - ti - na.____

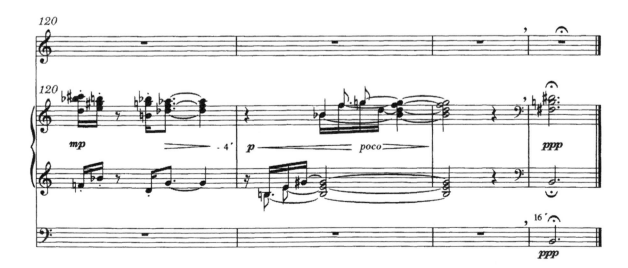

To John and Catherine Henderson

CHRIST'S BELL

(Carol Anthem)

Text
John Henderson

ALFRED HOLLINS
(1865 - 1942)

The great bells sound, now far, now near, And folks come eager-

*Malvern Chimes: First Quarter

** Second Quarter

COME, HOLY GHOST
(Whitsuntide)

Text
Latin, 9th Century
Trans. John Cosin

THOMAS ATTWOOD
(1765 -1838)

VERSE 1 [solo soprano or tenor, or semi-chorus]

Come, Ho - ly___ Ghost, our souls in - spire, and light - en

with ce - les - tial fire. Thou the a - noin - ting Spi - rit

art, Who dost Thy se - ven fold gifts im - part.___ Thy bless - ed unc - tion

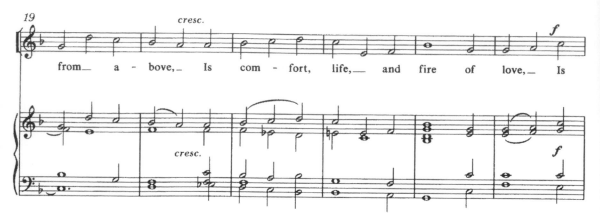

from_ a - bove,_ Is com - fort, life,_ and fire of love,_ Is

com - fort, life,_ and fire of love.

SYMPHONY

Sw.

Diaps.

Man.

VERSE 2 - Voices alone

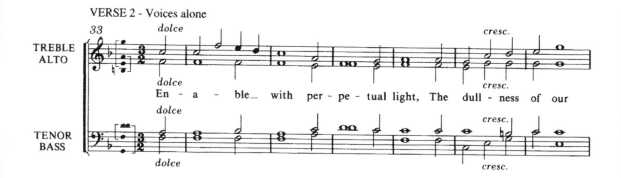

TREBLE ALTO

dolce *cresc.*

En - a - ble_ with per - pe - tual light, The dull - ness of our

TENOR BASS

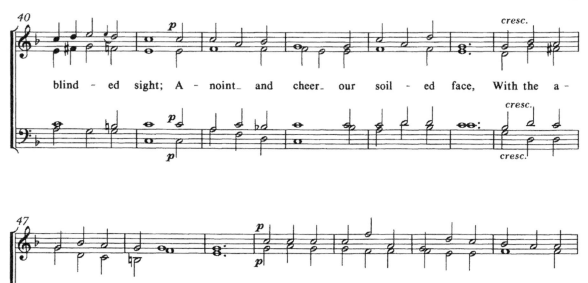

blind - ed sight; A - noint_ and cheer_ our soil - ed face, With the a -

- bun - dance of Thy_ grace. Keep far our foes,_ give peace_ at home,_ Where

Thou_ art guide,_ no ill can come; Where Thou_ art guide,_ no

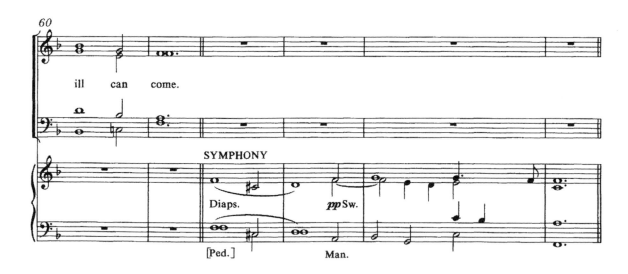

ill can come.

SYMPHONY

Diaps.

pp Sw.

[Ped.]

Man.

VERSE 3 - Chorus.

Teach us to know the Fa - ther, Son And Thee of

both to be but one, That through the a - ges

all a - long, This may be our end - less song;

[Man.]

Praise to Thy eternal merit, Father Son, and

merit merit,

[Ped.]

Ho - ly Spi - rit, Fa - ther, Son, and Ho - ly Spi - rit.

SYMPHONY

Sw. *mf*

Man.

COME, MY WAY, MY TRUTH, MY LIFE
(The Call)

Text
George Herbert
('The Call')

WILLIAM HARRIS
(1883 - 1973)

Come, my Way, my Truth, my Life! Such a Way as gives us breath, Such a Way as gives us breath, Such a Truth as ends all strife, Such a Truth, Such a Life

*This Anthem may be sung unaccompanied.

as kill-eth Death, Such a Life____ as kill-eth Death.
Such a Life____
Such a Life____

Come, my Light,___ my Feast,___ my___ Strength!___

Such a Light as shows a feast,
Such a Light,_____ Such a Feast as mends in
Such a Light,_
Such a Light as shows a feast,

length, Such a Strength as makes his

guest, Such a Strength as makes his guest.

Come,

Come my Joy, my Love, my Heart!

Such a Joy as none can move, Such a Love as none can
Such a Joy as none can move, none can Such a

part,— Such a Heart as joys in love,
Love,—

Such a Heart as joys in love.

In memory of Kenneth Leighton

ET RESURREXIT

Text
Nicene Creed;
George Herbert
('Easter');
Inchcolm Antiphoner

MARTIN DALBY
(b. 1942)

Et re-sur-rex-it_____ ter-ti-a di-e sec-un-dum scrip-tu-ras,

Commissioned by the City of Glasgow District Council for the Choir of King's College, Cambridge during Glasgow's year as European Capital of Culture, 1990.

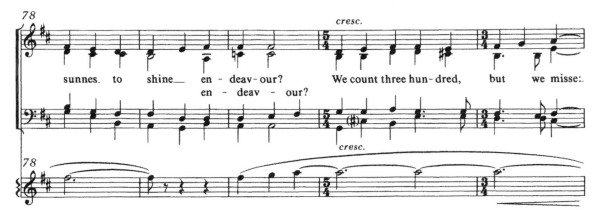

Teach it to sing Thy praise this day, And then this day my life shall date..

Ancora meno mosso

108 pp SEMI CHORUS

Cru-cem sanc-tam sub - i - it, qui in-
in -

FULL CHORUS

Al – le – lu – ia.

Al – le – lu – ia.

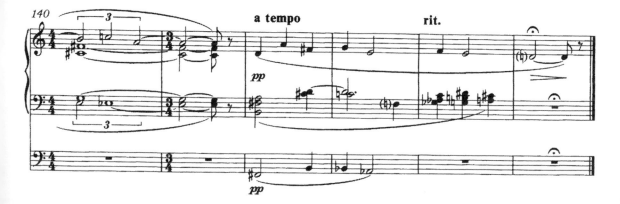

*For the Choir of St. Alban's, Tattenhall, on the occasion of
the Centenary of the rebuilding of the Parish Church*

FOR I WENT WITH THE MULTITUDE

Text
Psalm xlii, 4-7

PETER ASTON
(b. 1938)

Al - le - lu - i - a, Al - le - lu - i - a, Al - le - lu - ia.

Why art thou so full of hea - vi - ness, O my soul:

Man.

and why art thou so dis - qui - et - ed with - in me?

and why art thou so dis - qui - et - ed?

and why art thou so dis - qui - et - ed with - in me?

and why art thou so dis - qui - et - ed?

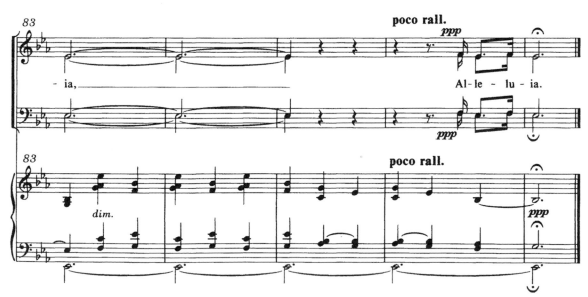

FROM THE RISING OF THE SUN

(Epiphany/General)

Text
Malachi i, 11

FREDERICK GORE OUSELEY
(1825 - 1889)

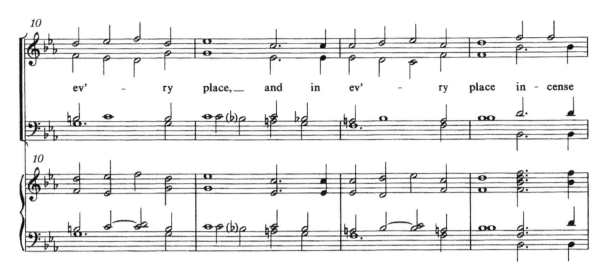

ev' - ry place,___ and in ev' - ry place in - cense

un - to___ my___ name:

shall be of - fer'd up un - to___ my name: for my

un - to___ my name:

un - to___ my name

name shall be great a - mong___ the hea - then, for my

a - mong___ the hea - then,

name shall be great a - mong the hea - then, thus saith the

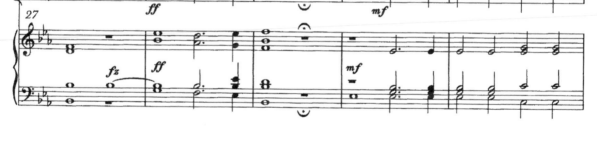

Lord, thus saith the Lord! From the ris - ing of the

sun un - to the go-ing down of the same my name shall be great, shall be

sun un - to the go-ing down of the same my name shall be

sun un - to the go-ing down of the same my name shall be great, shall be

sun un - to the go-ing down of the same my name shall be

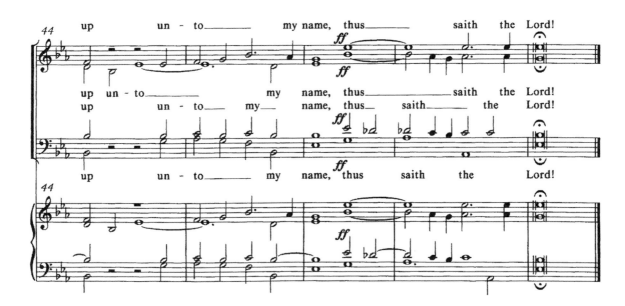

Specially composed for the wedding of Michael Pearce and Margaret Humphrey Clark,
St George's Church, Ashtead, Surrey, March 16th 1968

GRACIOUS SPIRIT

Christopher Wordsworth
(1807 - 1885)

SEBASTIAN FORBES
(b. 1941)

HOW BEAUTEOUS ARE THEIR FEET
(Saints' Days)

Text
Isaac Watts

CHARLES VILLIERS STANFORD
(1852 - 1924)

pro-phets wait-ed for, And sought, sought, but nev-er

found! How bless-ed are our eyes

How bless-ed are our

How bless - ed

That see this heav'n-ly,

eyes That see this heav'n - ly light! Pro - phets and

Ped.

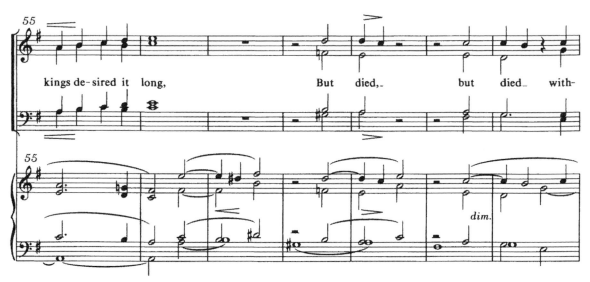

kings de-sired it long, But died,__ but died__ with-

- out_____ the sight. The Lord makes bare his arm_____ Through

all the earth a-broad; The Lord makes bare__ his__

The Lord makes bare his arm_____

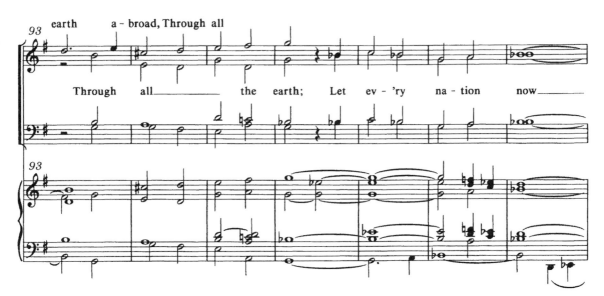

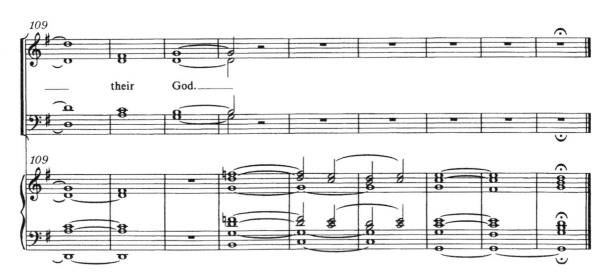

HOW BEAUTIFUL UPON THE MOUNTAINS

Text
Isaiah 1ii, 7

JOHN STAINER
(1840 - 1901)

SOPRANO: How beau - ti - ful up-on the moun - tains are the

feet of him that bring- eth good ti - dings, that pub - lish - eth peace that

ALTO: How beau - ti - ful up-on the moun - tains are the

* The small notes must be sung by *all* the parts if the passage is found too high.

HYMN TO THE TRINITY No. 1

Text
Kheruvimskaya Pesnya
(Cherubim's Song)
English adaptation by
W.G. Rotheby

PYOTR IL'YICH TCHAIKOVSKY
(1840 - 93)

JESU, GIVE THY SERVANTS
(Ave Maris Stella)

Text
Hymn to the Virgin Mary
English version by W. Chatterton Dix

FRANZ LISZT
(1811 - 86)

126

LIKE AS THE HART

Text
Psalm xlii, 1, 6, 15.

VINCENT NOVELLO
(1781 - 1861)

MARY LAID HER CHILD

Text
Norman Nicholson

JOHN McCABE
(b. 1939)

Text reproduced by permission of the author and David Higham Associates Ltd.

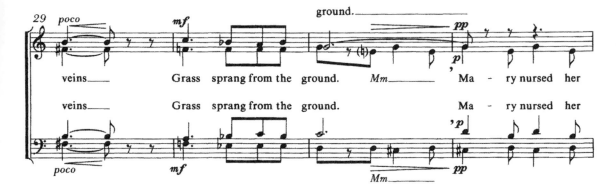

veins_____ Grass sprang from the ground. *Mm*_____ Ma - ry nursed her

veins_____ Grass sprang from the ground. Ma - ry nursed her

*Mm*_____

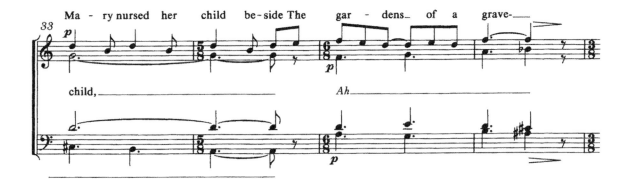

Ma - ry nursed her child be - side The gar - dens_ of a grave-_____

child,_____ *Ah*_____

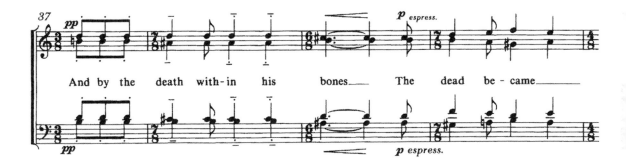

And by the death with - in his bones_____ The dead be - came_____

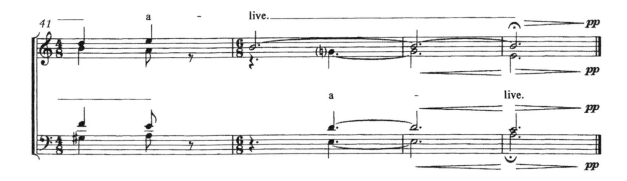

a - live._____

a - live.

To Ursula and Martin Watson

MY BELOVED SPAKE

Text
Solomon ii, 10-13

PATRICK HADLEY
(1899 - 1973)

Ped. 16 & 8 ft.

Score and parts for an orchestral version are available for hire from the publishers: 2+picc. 22(ca). 22/ 4231/ timp. perc./ hp./ stgs., or strings only with or without harp.

* The section, bars 10-21, if organ only is being used, should ideally be unaccompanied, but, should it be found advisable, some discreet assistance may be rendered by reference to the small notes. The large notes in this section refer to passages which occur in the full orchestral score.

Composed for the Thanksgiving Service held on August 8th 1965 in Sark
to commemorate the four hundreth year since the granting of the Royal Charter to the island.

O GIVE THANKS UNTO THE LORD

Text
Psalm cvi, 1-2, 4-6

ARTHUR BLISS
(1891 - 1975)

the no - ble acts, ___ the no - ble acts of the

- press the no - ble acts, ___

Ped.   Man.

Lord; or shew ___ forth his ___ praise, his ___ praise? ___

f

3

legato

Ped.

O LORD, OUR GOD, HOW GREAT IS YOUR NAME

Text
Psalm viii

ANTHONY MILNER (Op.43)
(b. 1925)

Commissioned for the Centenary of Royal Holloway College 1986

lips of chil-dren and of babes you have found praise to foil your e-ne-my, to

si-lence the foe and the re-bel. O Lord, our

God,_____ how great is your name thro' all the

144

God,_____ how great is your name thro' the earth,_____ how

great is your name!_____ I will give you glo-ry,

I will bless you day af-ter day,_____ and praise_____
I will bless you day af-ter day,_____ and praise_____
I will bless you day af-ter
O God_____ my king:_____
I will bless you

might, O God. Yours is an e-ver-last-ing

King-dom; your rule lasts for e-ver.

O Lord, our

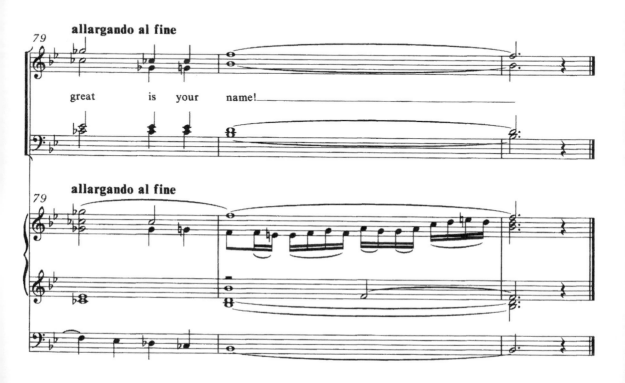

O MOST MERCIFUL

Text
Bishop Heber

ERNEST BULLOCK
(1890 - 1979)

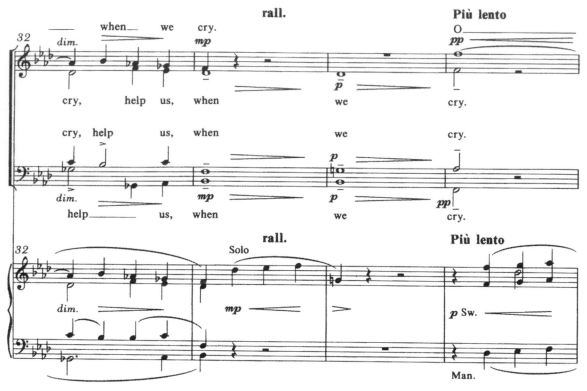

O QUAM GLORIOSUM

(All Saint's Day)

Text
Antiphon at first vespers
on the Feast of All Saints

PHILIP MOORE
(b. 1943)

Commissioned by the Friends of York Minster for their 1986 Festival

Note: After the first publication of this Book, the composer asked for a change in the words in bars 11-14 and his preferred version is printed here.

O STRENGTH AND STAY

Text
St. Ambrose
Translated by J. Ellerton

ERIC THIMAN
(1900 - 1975)

* Solo soprano or all sopranos

-da - tion_____ From hour to hour through all its chan-ges guide;

SOPRANO

ALTO

Grant_ to life's day a calm un-cloud-ed

Grant_ to life's day a calm un-cloud - ed

TENOR

BASS

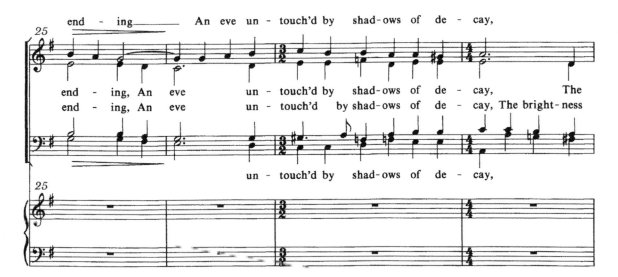

end - ing_____ An eve un - touch'd by shad-ows of de - cay,

end - ing, An eve un - touch'd by shad-ows of de - cay, The

end - ing, An eve un - touch'd by shad-ows of de - cay, The bright-ness

un - touch'd by shad-ows of de - cay,

Christ Thy co - e - ter - nal Word, Who, with the Ho - ly Ghost, by all things

liv - ing Now and to end - less a - ges art a dored.

A - men, A - men.

174

PRAISE YE THE LORD

Psalm cxlviii, 1-5

MICHAEL HURD
(b. 1928)

© Copyright 1966 Novello & Company Limited
This edition © Copyright 1996 Novello & Company Limited

Commissioned for the Choir of St Lawrence, Alton, to celebrate the rebuilding of the Organ. October, 1966.

Dedicated to the Rev. A.E. Fleming, M.A. Precentor of Gloucester Cathedral.

PREVENT US, O LORD

Text
Collect after the Offertory

HERBERT BREWER
(1865 - 1928)

Composed for the Gloucester Diocesan Choral Festival, June, 1900.

glo - ri-fy, we may glo - ri-fy Thy ho - ly Name,

Name, and

glo - ri - fy Thy ho - ly Name,

and fi-nal-ly by Thy mer - cy ob -

and fi - nal-ly by Thy mer - cy ob - tain ev - er -

fi-nal-ly by Thy mer - cy ob-tain ev - er - last - ing

Thy ho - ly Name, and fi-nal-ly by Thy

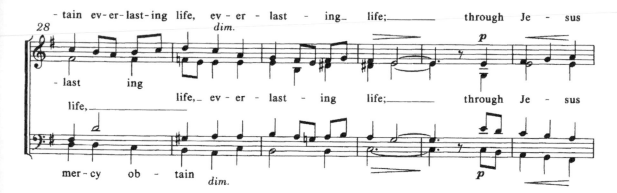

-tain ev-er-last-ing life, ev - er - last - ing life; through Je - sus

- last ing life, ev - er - last - ing life; through Je - sus

life, mer - cy ob - tain

Christ our Lord. A - men, A - men.

Christ our Lord. A - men, A - men, A - men.

Christ our Lord. A - men, A - men, A - men.

Christ our Lord. A men, A - men.

REJOICE, THE LORD IS KING!

(Ascension/General)

Text
Charles Wesley

BRYAN KELLY
(b.1934)

Lord and King a - dore; Mor - tals, give thanks, give

thanks and sing, And tri - umph ev - er - more:

Lift up your heart, lift up your voice; Re - joice, a -

* VOICES alone ad lib.

he had purged our stains, He took his seat, he took his seat a-bove: Lift up your heart, lift up your voice; Re - joice a-
Re - joice,.

- gain a - gain, re - joice, re - joice, I say, re - joice.
a - gain I say, re - joice, a - gain, re - joice.

Man.

His_ king - dom, his_

king - dom, his_ king-dom can-not fail; He_ rules_ o'er earth_ and

heav'n;_____ The keys_ of death, of death_ and

hell Are to our Je - sus given: Lift up your

heart, lift up your voice; Re - joice, a - gain, a -

allargando

- gain, re - joice, re - joice, I say, re joice.

allargando

SING TO THE LORD OF HARVEST

(Harvest)

Text
Rev. Dr. Monsell

JOHN HENRY MAUNDER
(1858 - 1920)

praise; With joy-ful hearts and voi-ces, Your Hal-le-lu-jahs raise, By Him the roll-ing

sea - sons, In faith-ful or - der move, Sing to the Lord of Har-vest, A

song of hap-py love. Sing to the Lord of Har-vest, Sing songs of love and

praise, With thank-ful hearts and voi-ces, Your Hal - le - lu - jahs raise.

By Him the clouds drop fat - ness, The_ de-serts bloom and_
By Him the clouds drop fat - ness, The_

spring, The hills leap up in glad - ness, The_ val-leys laugh and_ sing, the_
de-serts bloom and_spring. The hills leap up in glad - ness, The_ val-leys laugh and_

praise, With thank-ful hearts and voi-ces, Your Hal - le - lu - jahs raise.

Andante espressivo (♩.= 52)
Soprano, Tenor or Baritone Solo*

Heap on His sa-cred al - tar The gifts His good-ness gave.— The

Andante espressivo (♩.= 52)

Man.

gold-en sheaves of Har-vest, The souls He died to save,— Your hearts lay down be-fore Him,

dim.

When at His feet ye fall,— And with your lives a - dore Him Who died to save us

rall.

* This passage may be sung by all the sopranos (or tenors), or may be divided, the first portion sung by soprano (or tenor) solo and the second by baritone solo or baritones.

sing to the Lord,   sing to the Lord of   Har - vest,   sing to the Lord,   sing to the Lord,

sing, sing _____ to   the   Lord, Songs of   love   and   praise.   Hal - le -
sing, sing to the Lord,   to   the   Lord, Songs of   love   and   praise.   Hal - le -

sing to the Lord,

poco rall.

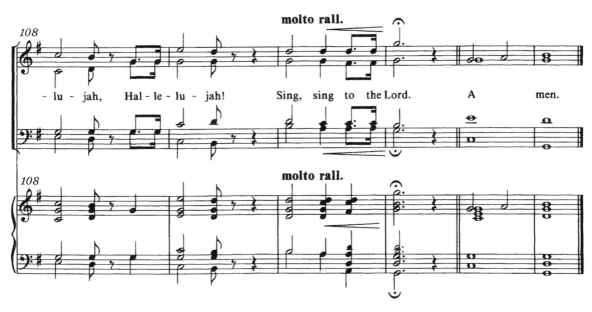

molto rall.

- lu - jah,   Hal - le - lu - jah!   Sing, sing to the Lord.   A   men.

SING YE TO THE LORD

(Easter)

Text
Exodus xv, 21, 4
and R. Campbell

EDWARD BAIRSTOW
(1874 - 1946)

for Ophelia Mary Adua

STARLIGHT
(Carol)

Text
Giles Swayne

GILES SWAYNE
(b. 1946)

Star-light is spread-ing a-cross the sky To-night: we're read-ing a mess-age by Star-light, and the mess-age is Love.

Love.

SOPRANOS descant *f*
3. Peo - ple of Plan-et Earth, Hear what I say:

ALL VOICES unis. *f*
div.
3. Peo - ple of Plan-et Earth, Hear what I say:

*VIOLIN

*Optional violin descant for repeat of verse 3.
Only repeat verse 3 if vocal descant is used.

THEY ARE AT REST
(Elegy)

Text
Cardinal J.H. Newman

EDWARD ELGAR
(1857 - 1934)

SOPRANO: They are at rest, they are at rest;— We may not stir the heav'n of their re-pose By rude in-vok-ing voice, or prayer ad-drest In way -

ALTO: They are at rest, they are at rest;— We may not stir the heav'n of their re-pose By rude in-vok-ing voice, or prayer ad-drest In way -

TENOR: They are at rest, they are at rest;— We may not stir the heav'n of their re-pose By rude in-vok-ing voice, or prayer ad-drest In

BASS: They are at rest, they are at rest;— We may not stir the heav'n of their re-pose By rude in-vok-ing voice, or prayer ad-drest In way -

(for rehearsal only)

To Clare and Keith

THEY ARE HAPPY

Text
Psalm xxxvi
('Grail' Translation)

JOHN JOUBERT Op. 119
(b. 1927)

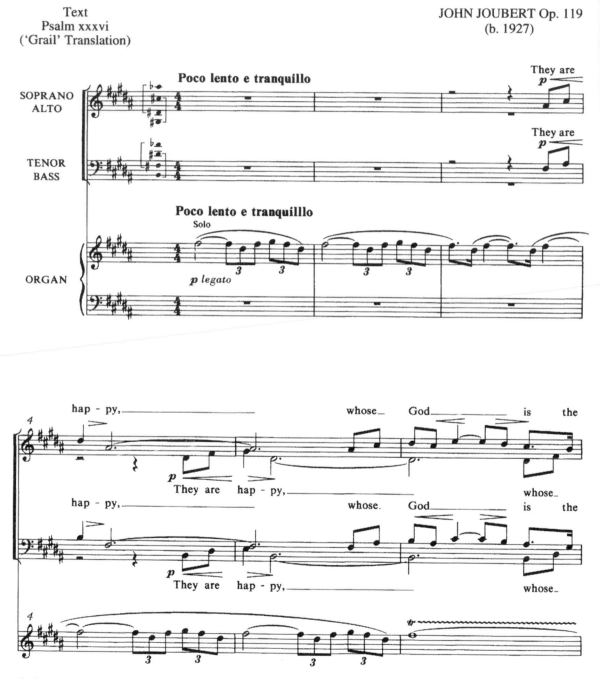

© Copyright 1996 Novello & Company Limited

For the wedding of Clare Faux and Keith Orrell at St. Chad's Cathedral, Birmingham, 30 July 1988.

The words of 'They Are Happy' are reproduced by kind permission of A.P. Watt Ltd. on behalf of the Grail, England.

THIS IS THE VOICE

Text
Walter Hilton

STEPHEN OLIVER
(1950 - 92)

This anthem may be sung by treble voices only, or men's voices only, or mixed voices as marked in the score.
The passage beginning bar 151 may be sung separately.

Commissioned by the Deanery of Nottingham, for the centenary celebrations of the Diocese of Southwell, February 1984.

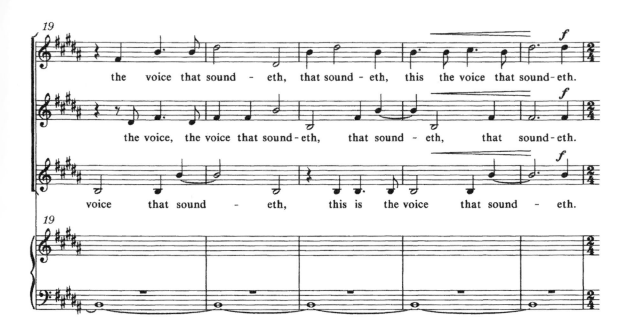

the voice that sound - eth, that sound - eth, this the voice that sound-eth.

the voice, the voice that sound-eth, that sound - eth, that sound-eth.

voice that sound - eth, this is the voice that sound - eth.

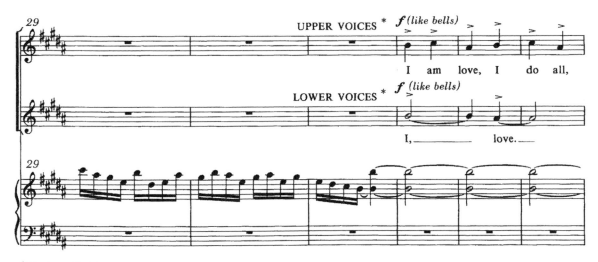

UPPER VOICES * *f* (like bells)

I am love, I do all,

LOWER VOICES * *f* (like bells)

I,_____ love._____

*Choir re-divides; men sing an octave lower.

UPPER VOICES   LOWER VOICES

do I love all, I am all love.___

do___ all___ love.___

Man.

I, love, do all, I love all love, do I

I,___ love___ do___ all___

love all love.___ This

___ for love.___ This

is the voice that sound - - eth.

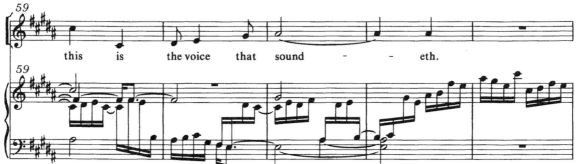

this is the voice that sound - - eth.

l'istesso tempo

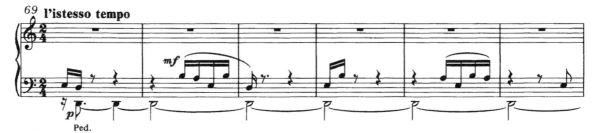

UPPER VOICES *mf dolce*

Good I give,— all good, all for love— I give

LOWER VOICES *mf dolce*

Good I give, all good,— all for love—

(Same manual as R.H.)

This is the voice that sound -

- eth, this is the voice that sound - - eth.

recit.
as fast as possible

(Full Organ)

*This may be at either octave, treble or baritone; in the case of mixed choirs, it may be sung by all the women or boys, using the small notes on bars 163 and 164 as a second part.

And yet be these called yours; I give them to you for love,

love. And yet be these called yours; I give them to you for

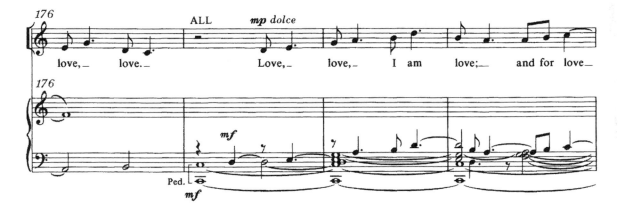

love, love. Love, love, I am love; and for love

ALL

mp dolce

mf

Ped.

mf

I do all that I do, and ye do nought.

I do all your good deeds, and all your good thoughts, and all your good loves

in you, and ye do right nought.

And yet be these called yours; I give them to you for love,

love. And yet be these called yours; I give them to you for

January 1984

THOU ART THE WAY

Text
G.W. Doane

CHRISTOPHER STEEL Op. 39
(1939 - 1992)

* or Tenor or Bass

* organ ad lib.

Thou art the Way, the Truth, the Life: Grant us that Way to know. That Truth to keep, that Life to win, Whose joys e - ter - nal flow.

THOU WILT KEEP HIM IN PERFECT PEACE

Text
Isaiah xxvi, 3,
Psalm cxxxix, 11,
I John i, 5, Psalm cxix, 175
and the Book of Common Prayer

ROBERT WALKER
(b. 1946)

Commissioned by the Dean and Chapter of Canterbury Cathedral for the Enthronement of Donald Coggan, 101st Archbishop of Canterbury.

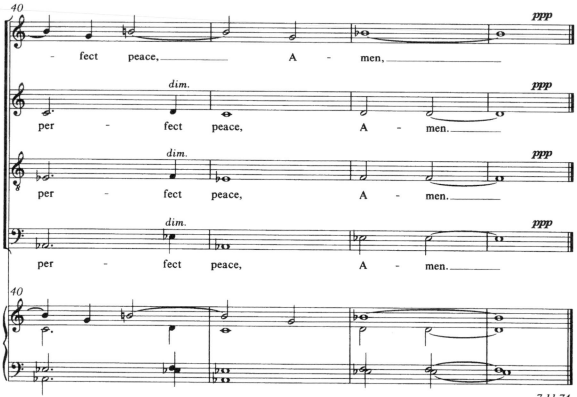

7.11.74

TU ES SACERDOS

Text
Psalm cx, 4 (Vulgate)

SAMUEL WESLEY
(1766 -1837)
Edited by John Marsh

Source

British Museum, ADD. MS 14340, in the composer's hand. This manuscript was presented to the Museum by Vincent Novello in 1843. *Tu es sacerdos* is dated 5 January 1814. It seems likely that it was composed for the Portuguese Embassy Chapel in London where Novello was organist and Samuel Wesley acted as his assistant.

Editorial Procedure

In this motet G clefs have been substituted for the original C clefs appropriate to the voices. The time-signature 𝄵 has been rendered 4/4. The composer's own dynamic marks 'piano' and 'forte' have been reproduced thus in full. Precautionary accidentals printed in small size have been added by the editor.

J.M. 1974

240

1) Tenor. 'In' omitted in the source

For M.M.

VIEW ME, LORD

Text
Thomas Campion

RICHARD LLOYD
(b. 1933)

If sung as an Introit, verses 2 & 3 could be omitted.

WHEN CHRIST WAS BORN

(Carol)

Text
Anon. 15th Century

Music
HAROLD DARKE
(1888 - 1976)